HIEROGLYPHS for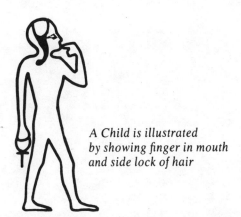

A Child is illustrated
by showing finger in mouth
and side lock of hair

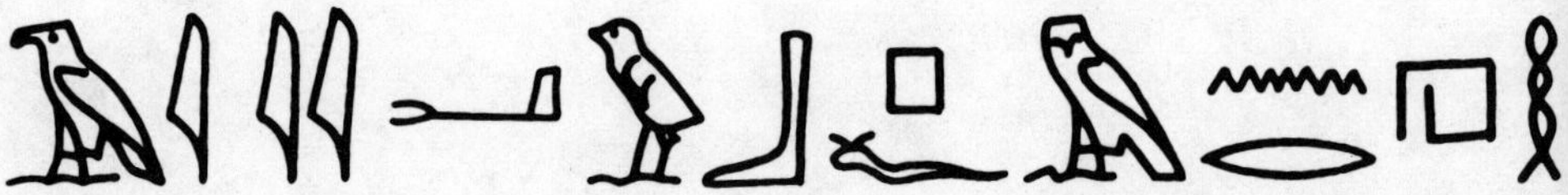

HIEROGLYPHS for fun

Your Own Secret Code Language

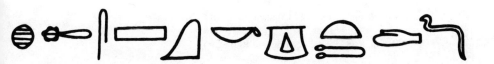

Joseph and Lenore Scott

VNR VAN NOSTRAND REINHOLD COMPANY
New York Cincinnati London Toronto Melbourne

*Dedicated to William Everett Scott and to
Arthur Kurtz, fathers of the authors*

First published in paperback in 1983
Copyright © 1974 by Joseph and Lenore Scott
Library of Congress Catalog Card Number 72-12443
ISBN 0-442-28168-4

Printed in the United States of America

Van Nostrand Reinhold Company Inc.
135 West 50th Street, New York, NY 10020

Fleet Publishers
1410 Birchmount Road
Scarborough, Ontario M1P 2E7, Canada

Van Nostrand Reinhold
480 Latrobe Street
Melbourne, Victoria 3000, Australia

Van Nostrand Reinhold Company Limited
Molly Millars Lane
Wokingham, Berkshire, England RG11 2PY

Cloth edition published 1974 by Van Nostrand Reinhold Company

16 15 14 13 12 11 10 9 8 7 6 5 4 3 2 1

Library of Congress Cataloging in Publication Data

Scott. Henry Joseph,
   Hieroglyphs for fun: your own secret code language.

   SUMMARY: Presents the basic "alphabet" of twenty-
four hieroglyphic letters with the approximate English
sound they represent and briefly discusses various
other Egyptian culture.
   1. Egyptian language—Writing. Hieroglyphic—
Juvenile literature. 2. Ciphers—Juvenile literature.
3. Egypt—Civilization—To 332 B.C.—Juvenile litera-
ture. |1. Hieroglyphics. 2. Egyptian language—
Writing. Hieroglyphic. 3. Egypt—Civilization—
To 332 B.C.| I. Scott, Lenore, joint author.
II. Title.

PJ1097.S3   417'.7   72-12443
ISBN 0-442-28168-4

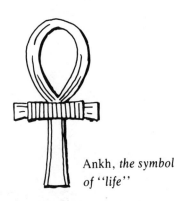

Ankh, *the symbol of "life"*

CONTENTS

PICTURE WORDS

Writing a message with pictures is very old, yet new too. Try making your own words with familiar objects. For instance:

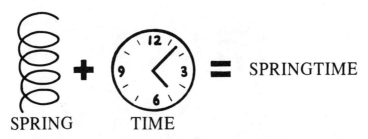

SPRING   TIME   SPRINGTIME

A puzzle or idea using pictures this way is called a *rebus*. If you reveal a message by performing personal actions, such as waving your hands and moving your body, that is *charades*. If you smile or frown, there are no sounds, yet it says what you feel. This is known as *body language*. There are many ways of communicating, besides using written words.

The Egyptians created a method of using pictures to tell messages thousands of years ago. The earliest samples were probably written on wood or reeds which have since disappeared. Pictures scraped on the surface of limestone slabs probably wore or washed away, with the passage of sandstorms and rain. So by the time someone finally carved some picture words into stone it was late in the development of the language—about 3000 B.C.

The origins of the Egyptian writing could have been in the way you might do it in English, as to write the word *belief*, pronounced bee-leaf, which is the same as the desired word, "belief".

Some Egyptian words started out perhaps with an ordinary sound, or everyday expression. If your throat were being examined by a doctor, you would say: Ahhhhhhhh. Since the mouth made that sound, why not use the shape of the mouth 𓂋 to represent that sound? That is how some pictures were selected.

With enough years, the original sound of an Ahhhhhhh, which sounds similar to Ahhhrrrr, gave Egyptians the idea that in any sound where the sound of an R was desired, the picture of a mouth would serve the purpose. So 𓂋 became a letter of the alphabet representing R. In time, words using 𓂋 often had nothing to do with a mouth at all.

The same is true for the rest of the Egyptian alphabet. Occasionally a picture might serve the original purpose, and be a part of the alphabet too. For instance, the wavy 𓈖 represents their word for water, but it also is the alphabetic letter N. How the sound N was selected thousands of years ago, based on 𓈖, is unknown.

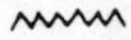

PICTURE ALPHABET

Actually, the picture writing of ancient Egypt is similar to English in many ways. Both languages are based on an alphabet. This book shows you the 24 basic letters of the ancient Egyptian hieroglyphic alphabet, plus numerous other illustrations they used.

In the Egyptian alphabet, the letter "S" is written ⌐ . An "A" is represented by a vulture 🦅 . To write an "M", draw the familiar owl 🦉 . So if you want to write the name *Sam*, you can do it this way:

S   A   M

Try writing *Mary*. M is the owl 🦉 . A is the vulture again 🦅 . R, as you remember, is the shape of your mouth ⌖ . Y is pronounced in *Mary* as though it were *ee*. In hieroglyphs, this is best illustrated by the picture of two reed leaves 𓇌 . *Mary* can be written in hieroglyphs this way:

M   A   R   Y

Also, you will soon see that both English and ancient Egyptian writing had symbols to represent a few of the ideas in a quick, short, clear way. English has symbols such as % $ & £ ¢ + = #, representing percent, dollars, and other words. The Egyptians also had their ways of writing more quickly. A number of the ancient pictograms represented entire words, rather than just one or two letters of the alphabet.

24 LETTERS

When you were four or five, you learned the English alphabet. Do you remember how much fun it was to recite quickly from A to Z? Now you do it automatically, and have gone along into new areas of conquest. Learning and using the Egyptian alphabet can be just as much fun, and take you further into new and interesting kinds of adventure.

The basic alphabet of ancient Egypt had 24 letters. Suppose you were a student or a scribe of 5,000 years ago. The teacher might say "Write the alphabet". Here is how it would look:

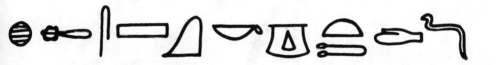

Wow! How do you remember a bunch of pictures like that! An imaginative scribe would probably use an ancient trick of memorizing that is still used today. The secret is to invent a story so that each picture has a part, and comes at the right time in the tale.

On the following pages is a story that presents the hieroglyphic alphabet in its correct order. You can use this method, if you like. Or, you might have fun inventing your own story. Anything that aids you in learning this ancient alphabet is worth trying. Notice how the story which follows uses the same pictures as shown above, and in the same order.

One hot and balmy day
an Egyptian <u>vulture</u>

Pronounced: a (hot, balmy)

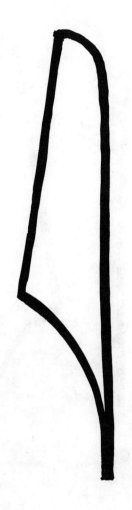

was sitting by a <u>reed leaf</u>,

feeding greedily on a
pair of <u>reed leaves</u>,

Pronounced: ee (feeding, greedily)

when he saw a man's dark arm with outstretched hand

smooth the wings

of a <u>baby quail</u>

Pronounced either: w (wings); or oo (smooth)

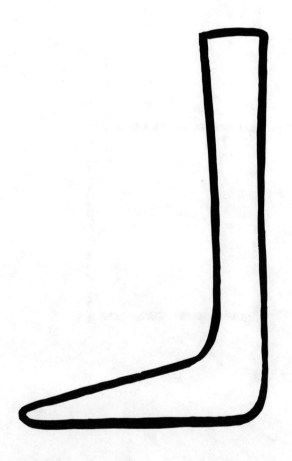

that bravely bobbed

near his <u>foot</u>

on a pink and purple

woven grass <u>mat</u>,

Pronounced: p (pink, purple)

while a fearsome

fanged horned viper

maliciously mesmerized

a mummified <u>owl</u>

Pronounced: m (maliciously, mesmerized, mummified)

nesting near the <u>water</u>.

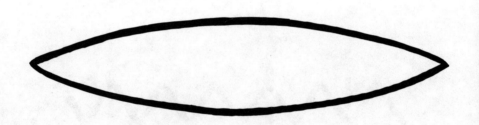

In the owl's red <u>mouth</u>

Pronounced: r (red)

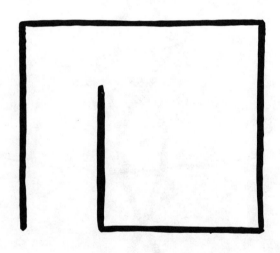

as it hopped through a
hay-filled <u>shelter</u>

Pronounced: h (hopped, hay)   23

was half a hank of

twisted flax,

Pronounced: h! (half, hank)—say fast, as in Ha!

**which it locked up in
a nearby <u>shallow hole</u>,**

Pronounced: kh (locked)—rhymes with Scotch "loch"   25

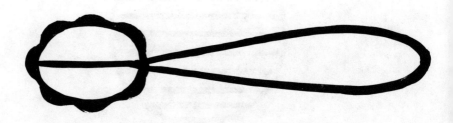

where a cow with an ochre-colored udder and tail

Pronounced: ch (ochre)—as in German "ich"

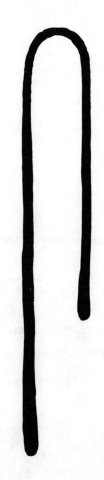

was standing under
a folded cloth

alongside a shady <u>pool</u>

Pronounced: sh (shady)

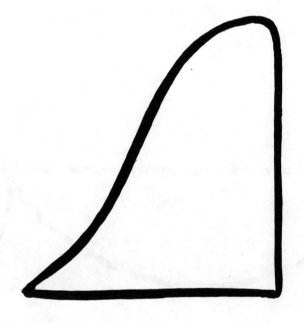

at the top of a

queen-sized <u>hill</u>

where a king-sized
basket with a handle

Pronounced: k (king)

rested on a golden jar <u>stand</u>

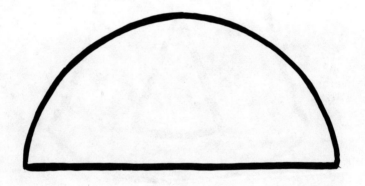

along with a

tasty <u>loaf of bread</u>

Pronounced: t (tasty)

on which the cow munched,

held back with a check-<u>rein</u>,

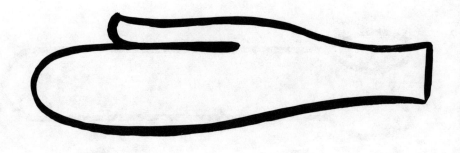

by a man with a dirty <u>hand</u>,

Pronounced: d (dirty)

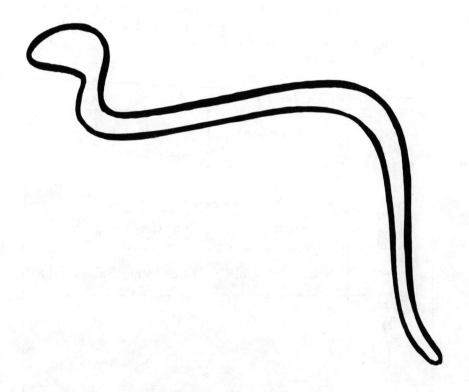

from stepping on a

nearby edgy <u>cobra</u>!

PRACTICE YOUR DRAWING

If you remember the pictures on the previous pages, you know the basic Egyptian alphabet. And if you can draw the illustrations too, you are making great progress. Try using tracing paper at first, if it helps you. The ancient scribes spent years copying and writing hieroglyphs, so don't expect perfection immediately.

It is important to know how the letters were pronounced. So remember that part too. Here is a handy list of the signs shown thus far. The sounds are the nearest to which the English language can come in duplicating the original speech.

HIEROGLYPH	REPRESENTS	PRONOUNCED
	vulture	a (hot, balmy)
	reed leaf	i (sitting)
	two reed leaves	ee (feeding, greedily)
	arm and hand	a (dark, arm)-"a" is gargled
	baby quail	w (wings); or oo (smooth)
	foot	b (bobbed)
	mat	p (pink, purple)
	horned snake	f (fearsome, fanged)
	owl	m (maliciously, mesmerized, mummified)

HIEROGLYPH	REPRESENTS	PRONOUNCED
water	n (nesting, near)
mouth	r (red)
shelter	h (hopped, hay)
twisted flax	h! (half, hank)—say fast, as in Ha!
shallow hole	kh (locked)—rhymes with Scotch "loch"
udder and tail	ch (ochre)—as in German "ich"
or	folded cloth or door bolt	s (standing)
pool	sh (shady)
hill slope	q (queen)
basket with handle	k (king)
stand	g (golden)
loaf	t (tasty)
rein	tj (check)
hand	d (dirty)
cobra	dj (edgy)

USE YOUR IMAGINATION

Note that some sounds seem similar to others. A few of the letters to which you are accustomed in English do not appear in the ancient Egyptian writing. That poses some problems, occasionally. When using hieroglyphs to represent English sounds you will sometimes have to use your imagination.

Visualize the nearest sound that can be made out of existing letters of the Egyptian alphabet, even if you have to combine them, or slur the sound. Often this mixup in pronunciation gives the desired effect.

In the ancient language there were vowels, such as are now used in English: *a, e, i, o, u*. However, the Egyptians did not write these sounds, even though they were spoken. This is not uncommon, since it happens in numerous Semitic languages.

Some of the letters may seem to be vowels, but were actually used differently in the original language. Scholars many years ago decided that when a word is not pronouncable because nobody really knows the correct original vowel sound, an *"e"* can be added for convenience. Therefore the acceptable way to pronounce ⟨glyph⟩ *fw* is to say "few" or "foo", even though that may not have been the original sound. There is more information about sounds in a later chapter on "Pronunciation".

For practice, use the basic alphabet to start writing some names or words. There is more than one way to write certain words. Combine the Egyptian characters to get the sound you want. If your picture-words differ from the samples shown here, or that which is done by other people, don't let it bother you. Your version can be just as good, especially if you or someone else can read the words so they sound about the way you intended.

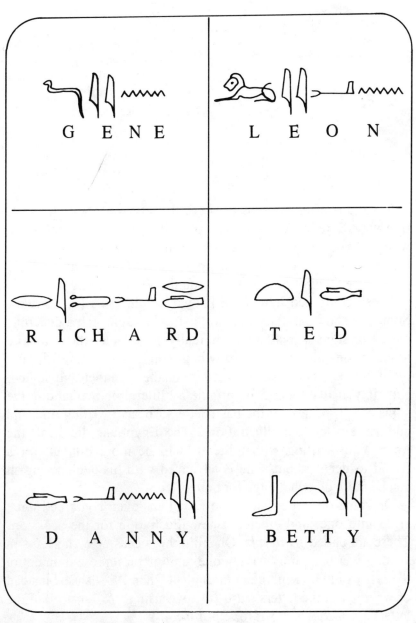

USE OF ALPHABET TO CREATE NAMES

Note: The closest sign to letter "L" is an "R", explained later in book

Combining two alphabetic
characters, w plus n
makes new biliteral wn,
meaning exist, or to be

Egyptians often combined two of the letters of their alphabet. In a way, it reduced the amount of writing needed to spell out a word. However, when such a combination was made, a new illustration was substituted for the original two pictures. There were more than 80 combinations commonly used in Egypt.

These combined letters are known as *biliterals* (*bi* for two). Some are shown in the following list. Although such a generous choice of signs is available, you really do not need them to write a name or any other word when you convert English into hieroglyphs. The original 24 letters of the alphabet will suffice. But, if you like, you can sprinkle a biliteral or two among the signs as substitutes for the basic letters, to save writing time and add variety to your illustrations. The Egyptians did it all the time. Your writing with biliterals will be more difficult for a friend to decode, but if he is advanced with his deciphering, it can be more of a challenge for both of you.

On some other occasions the Egyptians even combined three signs into one, and created a new illustration for the occasion. These are called *triliterals*. On still other occasions, shortcuts in writing were taken by having one hieroglyph represent an entire idea. It would be equivalent in English when "$" is used instead of writing out the letters *"d-o-l-l-a-r,"* using "&" instead of the letters *"a-n-d,"* or *"£"* for *"p-o-u-n-d-s."*

If you want to know *all* the ancient Egyptian hieroglyphic signs encountered by scholars, be prepared for years of study.

Three letters combine:
n *plus* f *plus* r, *to form*
single triliteral nfr,
meaning good, happy, beautiful

There are more than 3,000 that were used. Then, of course, you would want to know the quite extensive vocabulary of the Egyptians, with its accompanying complex grammar rules.

But as with English, only a small number of words or pictorial symbols were used in everyday writing.

ENGLISH SOUND	HIEROGLYPHS	BILITERAL	ILLUSTRATION REPRESENTS
ab			chisel or hairpin
adj			spool filled with twine
ak			cormorant
ba			wood ibis
dja			fire-making stick

41

ENGLISH SOUND	HIEROGLYPHS	BILITERAL	ILLUSTRATION REPRESENTS
gem			black ibis
ha			clump of papyrus
her			face
in			fish
ir			eye
ka			arms, extended
khen			skin of a goat
khet			branch
maa			sickle
moo			three water ripples
noo			bowl

ENGLISH SOUND	HIEROGLYPHS	BILITERAL	ILLUSTRATION REPRESENTS
pa	□ + 𓅓 =	𓅭	pintail duck, flying
per	□ + ⬯ =	⬜	house
roo	⬯ + 𓅓 =	𓃭	resting lion
sa	𓏤 + 𓅓 =	𓅰	pintail duck
sha	▭ + 𓅓 =	𓇆	pool with lotus flowers
shoo	▭ + 𓅓 =	𓆄	feather
soo	𓏤 + 𓅓 =	𓇗	Upper-Egypt plant
tja	⬯ + 𓅓 =	𓅿	duckling
wa	𓅓 + 𓅓 =	𓍯	lasso
wep	𓅓 + □ =	𓄋	horns of ox
wer	𓅓 + ⬯ =	𓅨	swallow or martin

WRITING SECRET MESSAGES

Egyptian hieroglyphs are great for writing messages that you don't want anyone else except your friends to read. The chance of encountering someone familiar with hieroglyphic writing is tiny. The words you use are based on the sounds of the Egyptian letters, though they will be, of course, English words. Knowledge of ancient Egyptian words is not really necessary unless you intend to be an Egyptologist some day.

Try reading the hieroglyphs given here. Where there is a space between the words, the Egyptians would normally have used what is called a *determinative*, which supplemented and clarified words. This resulted in continuous writing, without spaces. That is because in Egypt the determinatives separated the alphabetic parts of the words. Therefore spaces were not needed for an Egyptian to know when one word stopped and another began, as determinatives were a substitute for spaces.

You could make a huge project of trying to learn the several thousand determinative pictures, but it is not necessary. Leaving a space between words will serve your purpose just as well.

If you can read this message, you're becoming really informed, and should have fun with your new information.

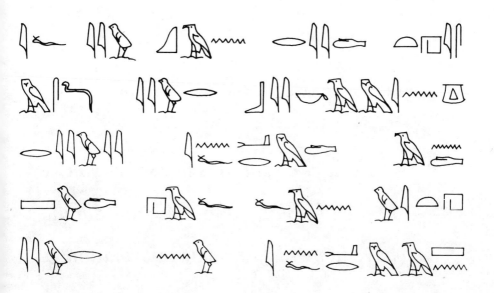

(See following page for interpretation)

45

Interpretation of the message on the preceding page:

"If you can read this message, you're

becoming really informed, and should

have fun with your new information."

As mentioned before, do not expect to find the *exact* equivalent in sound in Egyptian that you would desire in English. Use your imagination. Some slurring of sounds to simulate a desired sound is often necessary.

HIEROGLYPHS BY THE

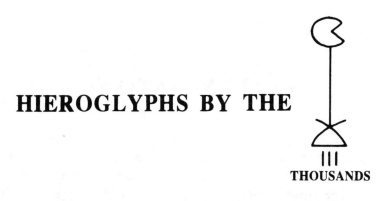

THOUSANDS

The picturesque alphabet and biliterals shown in this book are to help you change English words into picture substitutes. In such a way, you can write messages that very few people can read. You will also start to feel more at home when you see Egyptian hieroglyphs in books or in museum displays.

But the words you write, and the sounds you communicate, will naturally still be English. The ancient Egyptians had a completely different language using these same illustrations.

As you now know, the picture-signs of Egypt were supplemented with other symbols, not spoken, called determinatives. These extra hieroglyphs, some 3,000 of them, helped make the meaning of each word clear.

Take the word *pick*, for example. It can mean choose, or it might be a tool. As a tool, would you mean a pick axe for breaking hard dirt or rock surfaces? Or, perhaps you mean an ice pick, or even a tooth pick. You could also mean to remove fruit from a tree, take feathers from a chicken, daintily take small bites of food from a plate, dig at a pimple, seek flaws in an argument, or perhaps to steal money from a pocket, to start (pick) a fight, pluck (pick) the strings on a violin, use a pick (musical tool) on a guitar, find (pick) fault with someone, to tease (pick-on) somebody, to lift (pick-up) objects, or you might even mean the throw (pick) of a shuttle across a loom when weaving.

In ancient Egypt, supplemental signs helped avoid that confusion, and that is why the symbols that helped determine which definition was intended are known as *determinatives.*

DETERMINATIVES

One reason a list of determinatives is not given in this book is that they were unspoken additions to the original Egyptian words. Therefore you do not need them when using the ancient alphabet for writing English words. Secondly, what a task to learn all 3,000 of them! Whatever your struggle with English spelling and grammar, just think of the problem the ancient Egyptian scribes had when they studied their own language in school! Besides the hieroglyphs, they had an extensive set of grammar rules, requiring just as much study as any modern language.

Now you can see how Egyptians were able to make sense out of their writing when all the characters were written in continuous fashion, without spaces. Actually, the alphabetic symbols were followed by the explanatory determinative signs. Since the Egyptians knew which symbol was alphabetic and which was determinative, spaces were not necessary.

As mentioned before, you will be using spaces between words when converting hieroglyphs into English equivalents. This is because without determinatives you can not separate words properly.

In a way, the determinative signs of Egypt might be compared to your tone of voice when speaking English. When you talk, some words are said more strongly, some with emphasis at the beginning or end of a word, or others spoken softly. Some Southern belles in the United States, it used to be said, had thirty different ways of saying the word "Really," each with a different message to communicate. As a start, think of some ways yourself to show surprise (*really!*), a question (*really?*), chagrin (*REAL*ly), boredom (*reeee*ally), and see how many other variations and connotations you can find.

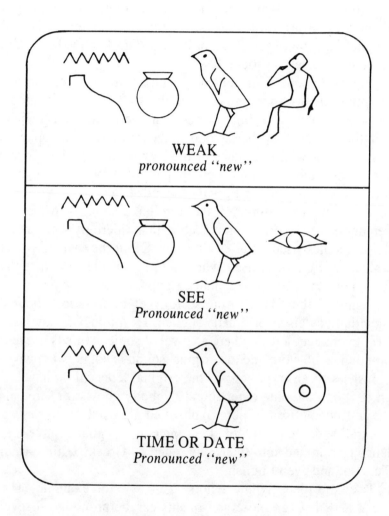

WEAK
pronounced "new"

SEE
Pronounced "new"

TIME OR DATE
Pronounced "new"

Although using the same alphabetic letters, the last sign changes. A completely different word results. These "determinatives" help determine the meaning that is intended.

PRONUNCIATION

While you now have some idea of the sounds of the Egyptian alphabet, the *exact* sounds of words as they existed in the original Egyptian speech is not known. Our knowledge today is based on a variety of sources.

When someone from the east, such as Mesopotamia, met an Egyptian, the Mesopotamian would try to write what he thought the Egyptian was saying, in his own Mesopotamian alphabet. But the words they heard may have been sounds spoken by someone not well educated, or the Egyptian could have had an accent or dialect from a certain part of Egypt. As a result, foreigners translated the Egyptian sounds in a variety of ways.

It is true that some of the foreign languages of Egypt's neighbors are more pronounceable than hieroglyphs, because those peoples used a fuller alphabet. Often they wrote vowels, which the Egyptians used when talking but did not write. The foreigners thus preserved many Egyptian sounds by using the foreign alphabet. Due to the scarcity of information about the Egyptian vowels as originally spoken, Egyptologists now use an "e" to connect letters where a vowel of some nature is needed to pronounce the word and the original sound is not now known.

Instead of an *e*, of course, the original letter might have been an *a, i, o, u* or some other sound. Nobody knows for sure, since the last people to use hieroglyphs died almost 1,500 years ago. Naturally descendants of the ancient Egyptians have other languages mixed into their own, such as Greek, Latin, Arabic, Turkish, and even English.

Take the hieroglyphic letters ⟨⟩ ⟨⟩ , for example. These are *g* and *d*. Even those consonants can be pronounced several ways, and nobody knows which one the old Egyptians actually used. A few of the possibilities are *eged, egad, egod, agod, god, goda, godo, geda, gead, gede,* or a number of other choices. Egyptologists today would pronounce it *ged*.

A *modern highway*
"hieroglyph"

PICTURES OF MANY KINDS

When travelers to Egypt started coming back to Europe many centuries ago with drawings of hieroglyphs, everyone was impressed by the stick figures they had seen on walls, monuments, pottery, and sculpture. They thought it was clever, and an ingenious way of conveying an idea through illustrations rather than words. It wasn't until the early 1800s, when the discovery was made that the ancient Egyptian language was based on an alphabet, after all.

The idea of using stick figures still appeals to anyone who wants to make a quick drawing. It is still the easiest way of communicating information to people who do not know your language. Some illustrated road signs form a universal picture language for drivers now. These road signs are common throughout Europe and many other areas, and beginning to become standard in the United States. The slash "/" across a sign means "Prohibited." So a slash across the letter "P" means "No Parking." A picture of an automobile with a slash across it means "No Automobiles Allowed." There are dozens of other picture symbols used throughout the world. A cigarette with an X across it of course indicates "No Smoking."

Look at some of the following figures used by the people of Egypt 2,000 to 5,000 years ago, and you probably will be able to guess what most of the symbols meant, even without knowing the language:

	WHAT IT SHOWS	USED WITH A WORD WHICH SAYS:
	seated man	man, or masculine
	man with hand in mouth	hungry, drink, speak, eat
	basket on head	to carry, to work
	arms tied behind	enemy, rebel
	man falling	to fall, to overthrow enemy
	child sucking thumb	young, child
	bent man with stick	old
	man with stick	strong, plunder, to teach
	walking man	messenger
	both arms raised	to rejoice, be high, mourn

	WHAT IT SHOWS	USED WITH A WORD WHICH SAYS:
	man with bow	soldier, army
	man upside-down	to be upside down
	man dancing	to dance, be joyous
	with stick and bundle	wanderer, stranger
	building wall	to build
	pounding mortar	to build, to pound
	with beard	a god, when with beard
	horizontal mummy	dead, sarcophagus
	legs walking	to approach, to walk
	walking backwards	to retreat, to turn back

Here are some additional hieroglyphs used in the ancient writing. Remember that sometimes the picture represents the animal or object shown. Other times the illustration was just added to a word for use as a determinative. At such times the meaning of the word could be quite different from what at first seems obvious, when you look at the picture. For example, a baboon 🐒 when used in ⟨hieroglyphs⟩ means "furious."

horse		hoopoe bird	
bull		ibis	
ass		heron	
pig		sparrow	
dog		duck	
jackal		duck (landing)	
hippopotamus		rabbit	
elephant		lizard	
ibex		crocodile	
monkey		snake	

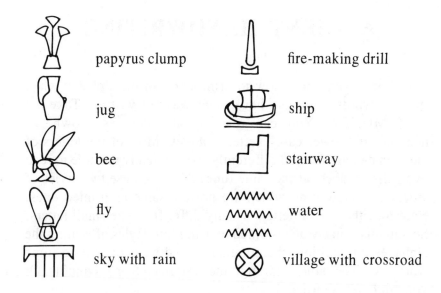

	papyrus clump		fire-making drill
	jug		ship
	bee		stairway
	fly		water
	sky with rain		village with crossroad

In fact, *most* of the hieroglyphs used by Egyptians had no sound! Typical illustrations were of people, gods, parts of the body, animals, birds, parts of birds, and reptiles. There were also pictures of fish, trees, plants, buildings, parts of buildings, ships, furniture, crowns, hunting equipment, warfare weapons, agricultural tools, baskets, jars, loaves of bread, rope, and many other items. Also, a number of the original objects illustrated are unknown now, even though the meaning of them is understood when used in a sentence.

Originally, most pictures represented a specific word, or idea. Eventually, the same picture might have been adapted for additional uses not related to the original idea. For example, in English or American usage, take the word *cat*. Initially and usually it signifies a four-legged furry animal. But now it can represent other things, such as someone especially flashy, causing others to comment, ''Look at that cool cat!'', which of course has nothing at all to do with cats. Egyptian usage often started the same way, so that pictorial puns or hidden original meanings in ancient hieroglyphs are common.

ANCIENT HANDWRITING

Although you know how to print letters of the alphabet when spelling words, you also have other ways of writing. Take the word MONEY. You can use capital letters as shown, or non-capital "lower-case" letters, *money*. Most of the letters of the alphabet are formed differently, so you really are able to read two full alphabets at the same time. Also, you use two styles of letters in handwriting which are not the same as printed ones. Here too, the capital letters usually differ from the small letters. So actually you are accustomed to using four styles of writing the alphabet. In addition, there are shortened ways of writing some words, such as *money*, through the simplified $ or £ symbols. Or you might use shorthand.

In the same fashion, a literate Egyptian who wanted to write a message usually found and welcomed shortcuts when using formal hieroglyphic signs. Easier handwritten versions eventually evolved. The first of these was the type now known as *hieratic*. Hieratic was used for many hundreds of years. Eventually that was simplified and shortened further, and later in Egyptian history another style came into use now called *demotic*.

Such shortened versions of writing were helpful for simple correspondence and business needs. Many papyrus scrolls employ that style, instead of the formal hieroglyphs. The hieroglyphic symbols shown in this book were generally for works of importance and permanence. Some places they were used were on monuments, tomb walls, building walls, sculptures and statues, official proclamations, burial areas, mummy cases, special documents, and religious articles.

Hieroglyphs are not used in Egypt today. The last person to write them regularly died almost 1,500 years ago. Important changes really began after the Greeks invaded Egypt in 332 B.C. Greek letters and words began to enter the Egyptian language. Three hundred years later the Greeks were followed by the

ENGLISH	HIEROGLYPH	HIERATIC	DEMOTIC
B	⏌	⌐	—
N	∧∧∧∧	⌐	—
H	⊓	⊓	₫
G	⬓	山	⌐
M	🦅	٤	٤

Romans just before the birth of Christ. Then came the Arabs, the French and the English.

Arabic is the official language of Egypt now. There is no relationship between Arabic and the ancient Egyptian language.

There are some remnants in Egypt, however small and changed, of the ancient language. This is in the literature of the Copts. The present Copts are primarily orthodox Christians. Even their older literature is a far cry from the original language as used at one time. *Copt* is based on the Greek word for Egypt, "Aiguptios." The end of the word, "guptios," which when slurred, is somewhat an approximation of the current word "Coptics." As the word implies, there is Greek in the language of later-day Egyptians of the old days, plus many other languages.

READING HIEROGLYPHS ALOUD

Among the letters in the Egyptian hieroglyphs which are associated with the alphabet, some sounds exist which are not found in English. As is true elsewhere, no two languages can be fully converted from one into the other. Each has special rules, and distinctive qualities. In the ancient Egyptian, to obtain the nearest English sound, you must sometimes slur a sound, or add an e between various letters to make them pronounceable.

In creating the L, as in *lion*, for instance, your imagination and a little intentional slurring of some sounds are needed. The nearest sound to an L is the *rw* of hieroglyphs, written as a lion ⟨glyph⟩ . Only through such substitution and slurring, for instance, can the names of *Cleopatra* and *Alexander* be converted into English. Those names are shown here because they were important in deciphering the famous Rosetta Stone, which was instrumental in solving the mystery of how to read the Egyptian hieroglyphs.

Similarly, a ⟨glyph⟩ can be either a D or a B, when speaking. This is because the two sounds are so similar in many words, as in "lab" and "lad." Therefore to read the name Cleopatra in the original language, the sound is nearer to being: *Kriowpadra.*

English pronunciation of the word for that ancient queen makes the name *Cleopatra* the acceptable sound, rather than the way the ancient Egyptians probably spoke it. (Did you know, by the way, that *the* famous Queen Cleopatra was actually the seventh famous Egyptian woman with that name? Six others preceded her, in Egypt's history.)

Therefore, when you go looking for a sound which you want, do not expect to find the precise one you seek when using hieroglyphs. Instead, pronounce a name or word as you normally hear it. Then look for the nearest Egyptian equivalent.

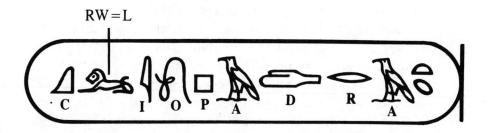

RW=L

·C   I O P A   D   R   A

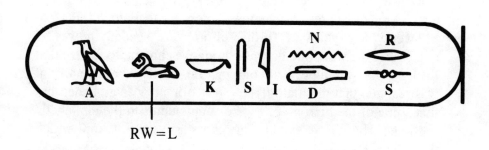

A   K S I D   R
                  S

RW=L

59

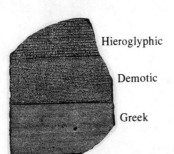

Hieroglyphic

Demotic

Greek

THE ROSETTA STONE

For many centuries the meaning of hieroglyphs was completely lost, since no one used them. Greek, Latin and Arabic, as well as other languages, began replacing the Egyptians' original speech. Finally, in 1799, during the French invasion of Egypt, one of Napoleon's officers found a flat stone with carvings at Rosetta, near the Mediterranean.

This particular stone at Rosetta was different from all others. Not only did it contain some hieroglyphic writing, but it showed two other forms of writing. They were recognized, before long, as being Greek and demotic, a late form of Egyptian writing.

Scholars suspected that the stone might have three versions of the same text. This turned out to be correct, and was the key to eventually discovering how to read the ancient hieroglyphs.

The Greek portion could be read easily. It explained that the stone was one of several placed in Egyptian temples to honor a Greek king of Egypt, Ptolemaios (Ptolemy), of about 200 B.C.

Twenty five years of further effort were needed, however, combining the work and findings of many scholars, to realize that the Egyptian writing was not one-picture-to-one-word. Finally, it was realized that the hieroglyphs were primarily an alphabet, but that some of the hieroglyphs were supplements to the alphabetic portions. This discovery became the starting point from which the extensive present knowledge of hieroglyphs stemmed.

Most famous and instrumental of the men to finally interpret the Rosetta Stone was a Frenchman, Jean Francois Champollion. He published his important findings when he was age 34, in 1824. Not only was he a genius, but he was a hard worker and instinctive scholar. At age 12 he was able to read French, Latin, Greek, Hebrew and Arabic. So the Egyptian challenge, which had waited 1,500 years to solve, was ready for him when he was ready for it.

DIRECTIONS FOR WRITING

Did you ever try writing backwards? Here is your chance. Egyptian hieroglyphs can be written and read in several directions. Any of the styles you try will be correct, since the Egyptians themselves used them all.

No matter how the hieroglyphs are written, just *read toward the faces*. For example, the words meaning "I am your father" should be read from the left to the right:

But, if you saw Egyptian written as in the following line, read from the right:

Notice that both sentences are the same. They just start from opposite ends. Normally, in Semitic-style languages, right-to-left is the customary direction. However, either direction is acceptable when using Egyptian hieroglyphs.

Sometimes you will even find that the writing goes downward, in a column. In such instances, read from top to bottom. And occasionally, as on the door of a tomb, the same writing may appear on both sides of the entranceway. At the right side the faces will normally look to the left, toward the door opening. On the left side the pictures are reversed so that the faces will look to the right instead, again toward the door opening.

FUN WITH NUMBERS

Want to be really different? Use ancient Egyptian numbers when keeping your bowling score, baseball statistics, football or basketball scores, or perhaps even when trying to confuse your mathematics teacher!

Interestingly enough more than 5,000 years ago, the people of the Nile had developed a numerical system which is much like our own, using 1, 10, 100, etc. In nearby ancient Babylonia, they used a system based on 60. Today's computers employ the binary method, based on 2, where each number is a combination of 0's and 1's. Here are the Egyptian numbers in their hieroglyphic form, and what they showed:

NUMBER	SIGN	SIGN REPRESENTS
1		a single stroke
10		bar used to hold oxen
100		coil of rope
1,000		lotus plant
10,000		finger
100,000		tadpole
1,000,000		man aghast at such a high number

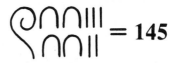 $= 145$

To use these numbers, however, sometimes takes a bit of doing. There were no written numbers for figures in between the main ones shown here. To write the number 4 took four individual strokes: ||||. Therefore, to write 145 you would have: ℚ∩∩||| . To write 1,623, do this: [hieroglyphs]

Writing fractions is something else again. Be glad you have decimals you can use, most of the time, instead of Egyptian fractions! To start, put a ⌒ (r) in front of the number. This indicates a number less than 1, or a fraction. Therefore 1/30th was written: ∩∩∩ or ⌒∩∩∩

Any fraction with a 1 in the numerator follows the same style, with a ⌒ followed by the number.

For 1/275, write: [hieroglyphs]

One-half has its own special symbol: ⊂ , and X = 1/4.

It is when you have a number higher than 1 on top that you can get complicated. For instance, 5-5/7 would be 5 plus a number of fractions that would add up to 5/7ths, yet have 1 on top as the numerator. Such numbers would be 1/2 plus 1/7 plus 1/14, which is 10/14. That reduces back to the original 5/7ths. So 5-5/7 is written: [hieroglyphs]

Want to divide 5-5/7 in half to 2-6/7? The least common denominator is 28, so you would have 2 plus 1/2 plus 1/4 plus 1/14 plus 1/28 (or, 2 plus 14/28 plus 7/28 plus 2/28 plus 1/28):

[hieroglyphs]

Things can get even more complicated. In a mathematical papyrus of about 1600 B.C., there is the number 2/61. Care to guess how it had to be written? The correct answer is 1/40 plus 1/244 plus 1/488 plus 1/610! In hieroglyphs, it is:

[hieroglyphs]

So, be glad you learned your arithmetic in the 20th century instead of in ancient Egypt!

EGYPTIAN STORY-TELLING

Everybody enjoys a good story. You liked them as a young child, and you appreciate a good one now. The characters change, the settings differ, and the action is of another kind. Sometimes the stories have been loaded with excitement and drama. Other times they are lovely tales that just make you feel good.

Egyptians were the same. They liked good stories. In the scribe's school pupils had the chance to copy stories they had heard from their parents, friends, or a passing traveler. As they advanced in school, the chance to write their own stories occurred. Sometimes older stories, like fables or fairy tales, had flourishes added by imaginative students. So long as they could practice their writing, that was an important part of their studies.

They were fond of tales of glory in battle. Sometimes the battles were against real people, sometimes against evil gods. They knew of adventure stories in which the Pharaoh or others would go on lion hunts, chase an enemy, take exciting sea voyages, or visit foreign lands. Some were quite realistic; others highly imaginative. When lettering formal hieroglyphs became cumbersome, sometimes students would switch to the faster handwriting style of hieratic or demotic script.

Remnants of some of those stories still exist in museums today. Usually the best stories and best-preserved samples are on papyrus rolls. Since papyrus was expensive, it was used by only the more advanced scribes, and on scrolls made for important occasions. Practice writing by younger students was generally done on limestone pieces, or pottery chips.

*The god Re Harakhti,
who plays a part
in the story of
"The Two Brothers"*

The famous Rhind Papyrus is a fascinating glimpse into the mathematics of ancient Egypt. Another papyrus tells about medical studies and cures, revealing that the physicians had a wide scope of knowledge, considering how many thousands of years ago it was written. There are also papyrus scrolls about the Egyptian gods and ideas about the creation of the world.

Of the ancient scrolls that still remain, one is about the adventures of Sinuhe the sailor, who led an interesting life in the eastern end of the Mediterranean Sea area. Another gives the Egyptian version of the Seven Lean Years in Egypt, about 2650 B.C. during the time of the Third Dynasty. It is not hard to see how the same story is related to the famous dream that Joseph interpreted for a much later Pharaoh in the familiar Bible story about fat and lean cows (years).

Still another papyrus which makes fascinating reading is one from about 1225 B.C. concerning two brothers, Anubis and Bata. (See next page.) The experience of one of the brothers parallels the Biblical story of Joseph in Egypt, and Potiphar, wife of his master. The story was quite popular, so numerous scribes copied it, often adding little variations to it.

Once upon a time there were two brothers. The older one, Anubis, did much to raise and train his younger brother, Bata. Bata, in turn became an excellent worker in care of the family's fields. One day when they were planting, Bata was sent back to the house to get more seeds.

It was then that trouble began. Sitting at home combing her hair was the wife of his brother. She started a conversation, flattering him by saying, "You have great strength. I see your strength and energy more each day."

Then she stood up, took hold of him, and said "Come, let us make love together. It will do you good, and I shall make some fine clothes as a reward for you."

Bata was furious. He had considered his older brother and his wife as honored parents. So he rebuffed her, saying, "Don't ever say that to me again. Let us forget you ever spoke of it."

Then he went back to the field. But Anubis' wife was afraid that Bata might tell of her unfaithfulness. So she messed up her clothes, bruised herself, and told Anubis that night that Bata had beaten her and taken advantage of her when he came at midday for the grain.

Anubis was wild with rage. He waited with sharpened knife inside the stable door, ready to slay Bata when he came back from the fields to put the cattle in the barn. But as Bata started to enter, the first cow said to him, "Your older brother is waiting to kill you. Run away."

Bata prayed to the god Re Harakhti to protect him. The god heard, and created a large body of water filled with crocodiles. This he used to separate the two brothers from each other. Through an act of sacrifice, Bata convinced Anubis of the truth, but he left anyway to go to the Valley of the Cedar. Anubis went home, where he covered his head with dust in remorse. Then he killed his wife, and began praying for the return and forgiveness of his brother.

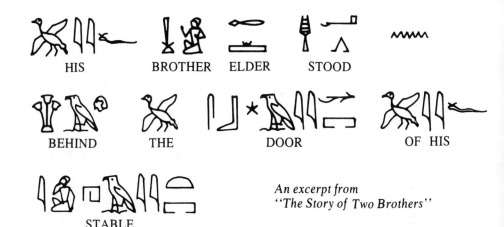

HIS   BROTHER ELDER STOOD

BEHIND   THE   DOOR   OF HIS

STABLE

An excerpt from
"The Story of Two Brothers"

In another extended version of the two-brothers story, Bata eventually becomes lonely, being away from home. So the god Re Harakhti creates a beautiful girl to become his wife. She, in due course, is discovered by the Pharaoh, who moves her to the royal residence.

In numerous incidents, the wife now seeks to destroy Bata. In each instance, his spirit returns. First he appears in the form of a powerful bull, beloved by everyone. But then his wife arranges to have the bull sacrificed.

Two drops of the bull's blood splash on the palace wall and develop into two beautiful trees soon worshiped by everyone. But again, Bata's wife shows her influence with the Pharaoh. She arranges to have the trees cut down. In the process, a wood chip flies into her mouth. She swallows it, and after many days she bears a child as a result. Again it is a reincarnation of the soul of Bata. The child eventually becomes the Pharaoh.

There are more details to the story. Perhaps the crowning touch is the way in which the scribe who wrote the papyrus finishes the manuscript. It probably represents the feeling of anyone who writes a novel or tells a story, even today. At the end of the papyrus scroll he pens: "Written by the scribe Anena, the owner of this roll. He who speaks against this roll, may Tahuti smite him!"

HOW TO GET LOST IN EGYPT

Here is a riddle the Sphinx might well have asked: "What is up when it is down, lower when it is above, and upper when it is below?" That ought not keep you guessing too long.

The answer is "Lower Egypt and Upper Egypt." That is because the Nile River flows northward into the Mediterranean Sea. When boats would sail down the river to its mouth, they were said to be headed toward Lower Egypt. Upstream was toward the source of the river which, being central Africa, was to the south. Therefore Lower Egypt is north, Upper Egypt is south.

Try another puzzle, based on this map of Egypt and the Bible lands. See if you can identify the names shown. The words used are in hieroglyphs, but when you pronounce them they give the English equivalent presently used. The small numbers next to the hieroglyphs are the keys to the answers, shown here if you want to refer to them.

1. Alexandria
2. Aswan
3. Cairo
4. Israel
5. Jordan
6. Libya
7. Mediterranean Sea

8. Nile River
9. Red Sea
10. Saudi Arabia
11. Sinai
12. Sudan
13. Suez
14. Thebes

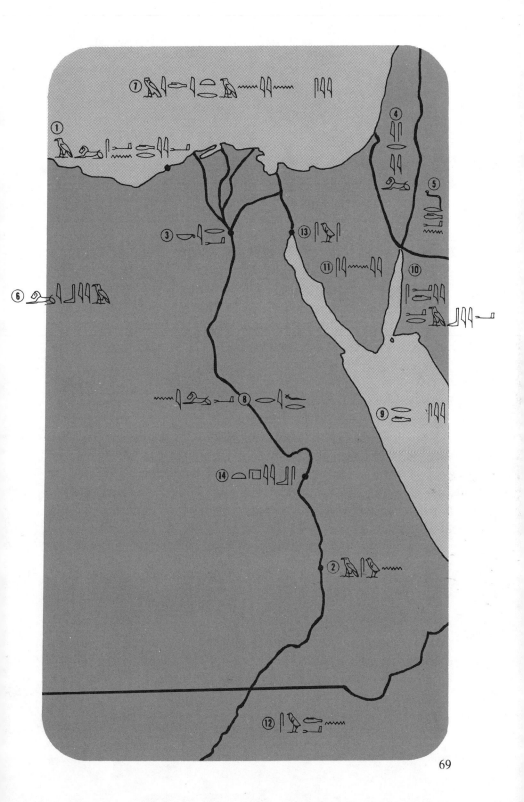

30 SQUARES

Among the most famous of the ancient Egyptian games is one which has a playing surface of thirty squares, 3 squares wide by 10 long. The game is called Senet.

In Egyptian, the biliteral *mn* not only is represented by a silhouette of the game board and its playing pieces, but was the word for "remain." Since remaining on the board is part of the strategy of Senet, use of a game-board hieroglyph as the sign for "remain" is quite appropriate.

Try playing this game of thirty squares. Here are instructions for making your own board, and for playing:

Players: Two persons

Board: Look at the illustration shown. Draw the playing surface of 30 squares on a large piece of paper. Or, you can make a more permanent board on a piece of wood, heavy plastic, or other material. Squares about 1½″ by 1½″ are a reasonable size, but they can be larger or smaller. It depends upon the playing pieces you have.

Mark the last five boxes along the bottom right edge as shown. The first mark ⚶ represents *nfr*, meaning "good." X stands for 4, in this game. The III, II and I mean 3, 2 and 1.

Playing Pieces: Ten playing pieces are needed for each player. All of the ten should be alike. The two players need different pieces so they can be easily distinguished. You might use red and black checkers. Or, two kinds of buttons, poker chips, coins, bottle tops, or any other small objects will do.

Move Selector: You can make your own move-selector, if you desire. It is a four-sided piece of wood, about a half-inch on each

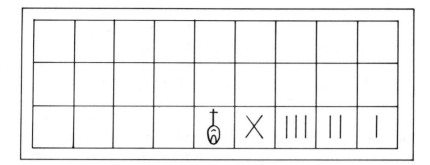

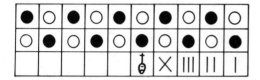

Set up board with
20 pieces as shown,
in alternate colors

side, and two to three inches along. Roll it, as you would a die. The four sides have one mark apiece: 1, 11, 111, 1111. No markings are on the ends. (If you want a move-selection method with less work, try four pennies. When you shake and drop them on the table, count the number of coins that are heads-up.)

To Start: Place your playing pieces in alternating colors along the two unmarked rows of ten squares. The illustration shows how this should look. When you roll the die, or count heads on the four coins, the number indicates the moves to be made.

Object: To move as many pieces of your own off the end of the board as you can, according to the rules of the game. The highest number off wins, but any of your opponent's pieces which you capture do not count.

Playing Rules: Instructions are based on the best reconstruction of rules that scholars have made. Egyptologists long studied written and illustrated references to the game, but no precise explanation has been discovered. Yet, the following rules fit, and make an interesting game.

1. Players alternate in taking one turn apiece.

2. All moves must be either up, down and/or lengthwise toward the marked end of the board. No backward or diagonal moves are allowed. A playing piece moves as many positions as

the die or coins show. Moves can be either in one line, turn a corner at right-angles, or a combination of the two.

3. The playing piece must either land in an empty position on the board or it must land on a space occupied by the opponent. In moving the number of squares called for, you count any in-between spaces, whether empty or occupied by a playing piece of either person. If you land on an opponent's square, the opposition's piece is captured and removed from the board. Your piece cannot be moved if it would land on a space already occupied by yourself.

4. Once a playing piece ends on a marked section of the board, it is safe from capture. However, the next play by the owner of that piece must be applied to it, if at all possible. To move a piece safely off the board requires an exact count. Thus, if a player is on II, he must have a 2 to move off the board. If he is on II, throws a 1, and the I is open, he must move there in preference to any other move. Only if the throw cannot be applied to any of your other pieces in a marked square can a move be used by another available playing piece.

5. As Rule 4 implies, a playing piece can first land on any of the numbered sections, such as I, II, III, X or ♀ . He is not required to begin at ♀ , especially since no backward moves are allowed.

6. Two pieces cannot occupy the same space, even in the five safe areas.

7. If a player throws four tails with his coins, he loses his turn. Also, if there are no moves a player can use on a given throw, he loses his turn. This sometimes occurs toward the end of a game.

8. Another game, if you find this one needing more strategy, is to add a rule that the game stops when one player has all his pieces off the board. At such time, then count each player's pieces that have moved safely off the end of the board. This makes the game especially interesting due to strategy in removing opponent's pieces before he can score, yet you try to score as many points for yourself as possible.

TO KNOW WHO'S (WHO)

As an ancient Egyptian, you would be among the chosen few if you wrote your name, then put it in an oval. The oval itself is called a *cartouche*. It was the drawing of a loop of rope, with the two ends sticking out at the end. This oval was reserved for the names of pharaohs, queens and royal personages. The Pharaoh Kufu (or Cheops, as he was known in Greek), wrote his name this way:

K   U   F   U

To tell whether a name was masculine or feminine, you can follow the style of the Egyptians. After a man's name, add the picture of a man . For a woman, the sign would be . However, female names generally used a ⌒ (*t*) after the name, rather than the illustration for woman.

A few more things about ancient Egypt might also interest you. Despite occasional changes, even the earliest writing was understandable to persons born 3,000 years later. It is now only 700 years or so since Chaucer wrote his Canterbury Tales in England, yet how difficult it is to understand and interpret this relatively recent English writing! Even the original texts of Shakespeare's plays, less than 400 years old, can be slow reading.

Did the Egyptians have a grammar, as English, French, German, Spanish or any modern language does? Yes indeed. It was an excellent, well-developed one, which you can study when you get into advanced Egyptology.

Don't worry about your spelling, if you are writing with the hieroglyphic symbols. The Egyptians themselves had various ways of spelling the same word. Even in the famous Rosetta Stone, the word "writing" occurs four times in one of the lines, and is shown in four variations. Perhaps the Egyptians were taught to avoid repeating themselves in the same sentence or paragraph, just as you are presently taught in school.

Sometimes you hear the word *hieroglyph,* and other times *hieroglyphic* or *hieroglyphics.* These words are not interchangeable if you want to be correct.

Hieroglyph is a noun, such as the *cold* in "I have a cold," or *writing* as in "Look at my beautiful writing."

Hieroglyphic is a descriptive adjective. It describes what kind of writing is being done. In this instance it is *hieroglyphic* writing.

So if you want to be correct, say you draw or write a *hieroglyph,* or know how to write *hieroglyphs.* But, when you do this, or read the original language, you are involved with *hieroglyphic* writing.

Therefore, it is *not* right to say, "I am writing *hieroglyphics.*" You may hear and see this word misused many times, but that still does not make it correct.

The scribes who wrote hieroglyphs worked hard to be neat. They kept their characters in eye-appealing balance. When two flat characters were to follow each other, it was quite proper to place one over the other. In this way two flat symbols would be nearer in height to the tall one next to them. For example in the word *strides:*

Sometimes you will see Egyptian writing with three small lines under a character ||| . This is the symbol for "many" or "a multiple of". The illustration therefore means "many men."

INTERESTING HIEROGLYPHS

 A playful kitten can be loving and a lot of fun. But when it grows up to be an adult cat, it usually becomes aloof, with a self-centered personality of its own. Seeming so independent, and looking so unconcerned at the many things going around it, the cat has given a regal impression for many centuries. The Egyptians of 5,000 years ago were just as aware of this. They reasoned that perhaps the cat was really a god. So they worshipped it as such. A cat-goddess was known in ancient Egypt as the god *Bastet.* But the wonderfully surprising name by which the Egyptians called all cats was , which properly pronounced comes out with the sound *meow!*

 Want an easy way to show the word "hear," or "listen," in one picture? The Egyptians merely drew an ox's ear.

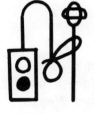 Writing in ancient Egypt was done usually in two colors, red and black. The red served to mark the end of a sentence, and occasionally to indicate the names of deities. Black served for most other uses. The hieroglyph at the left shows the brush-case for holding the writing brushes, a pot of water to wet the ink, and a palette to hold the black and red paint. All three items were held together with a string for easy carrying by the scribe. Some hieroglyph writing used other colors too, as blue, yellow, or the natural hue of the object illustrated.

This is the hieroglyph for a roll of papyrus, tied by a ribbon with a bow. Papyrus was expensive, and not to be wasted, because of the labor required to make it. The sheets were made from papyrus reeds, about one-foot long. Two layers of the reeds were squeezed and dried together at right angles. Then the sheets of papyrus were joined together. One roll still in existence is 130 feet long. The writing side usually had the reeds running horizontally, to make the writing easier. Although our present word *paper* comes from *papyrus*, today's paper is usually made from wood or cotton fibers, rather than reeds such as the Egyptians used.

Here is a familiar symbol you see worn as an amulet or good luck charm, even today. In ancient Egypt it represented the word "life," or "long-life." You will see it in many Egyptian illustrations, in the names of gods and pharoahs, and in hieroglyphic writing. The illustration itself is that of a sandal strap.

It is not known why this little sparrow had a bad reputation. Perhaps if this bird did not inherit the honor, another symbol would have been found anyway. Possibly the sparrow was the one which would peck at the freshly planted seeds of the hard-working farmers, damaging their crop. The sparrow's hieroglyph is the one used in words meaning bad, defective, empty, ill, and perish.

The sign meaning "good," and words related to it, is a heart and windpipe. In the original Egyptian the word was *nfr*, or *nefer*. The famous statue of the beautiful Eighteenth Dynasty Queen Nefertiti makes good use of the word, as part of her name.

These words represented to ancient Egyptians what the word "English Language" means to you. However, since the occasions on which the inhabitants of the Nile River country usually saw hieroglyphs was in official or religious situations, they felt that the writing was of sacred origin. The pronunciation of the signs shown is *Medew Neter*, or "The God's Words." Actually the words read *mdw ntr*, so that a number of other ways of speaking the words in ancient Egyptian are possible.

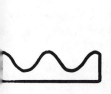

If you think that the expression "to go west" (meaning: to die) came from the old Western movies, you're thousands of years behind the times. In ancient Egypt, burials were done where the sun would sink into the earth. That, of course, was the West. Usually this put burials among the hills and sandy country away from the green cultivated area of the Nile River. The word *west*, in hieroglyphs, included the symbol: ◠◠◠ , meaning desert or sandy hill country. The same sign is used in the word for tomb and necropolis. So the concept of having the deceased's body and soul "Go West" is at least 5,000 years older than the movie version.

MORE THAN WRITING

Besides introducing the important idea of writing information in the picture form of hieroglyphs, the ancient Egyptians are known for other important developments. They invented a solar calendar of 365 days. They worked out an elementary form of arithmetic, based on multiples of 10. They were also the first known to evolve a real study of human anatomy, sickness and medicine, impressive even by the modern definition of those words.

They made great pyramids and buildings from huge stone blocks, yet had only simple copper and stone tools. They had no wheels, yet with ropes, ramps, rollers and human muscle power, created the world's largest stone structure, the great Kufu pyramid, which has endured for about 4,000 years.

PERPETUAL LIFE

Egyptians had the feeling that hieroglyphs possessed the spirit of whoever the writing was about. "The Gods' Words," they called it. As such, a person would live on into eternity when his name was inscribed in hieroglyphic writing.

Sometimes the reverse took place. If someone was disliked, his or her name could be scratched out or chiseled away wherever it was carved. At that moment, immortal life-after-death came to an end. The same was true with sculptures or portraits of a deceased person. Wholesale destruction of a pharaoh's name sometimes occurred when the next monarch sought to wreak vengeance upon the memory of the dead ruler.

In mummy and tomb writings, some animals were drawn without legs or heads. This was so the animals would not wander away. With this done, the deceased's spirit had enough to feast upon, into eternity.

AÏDA

Going to a performance of the great opera about Egypt, Aïda (pronounced 𓄿𓇋𓂧𓄿) is something you may now want to do, or maybe even have already done. Doubtless you have heard the famous Triumphal March from Act Two many times on the radio, or played as the entrance march at school graduations. Giuseppe Verdi wrote this spectacular musical pageant in 1869 to help commemorate the opening of the Suez Canal.

In the stage scenery of the opera you may well see painted hieroglyphs and authentic styles of ancient Egyptian costumes for both men and women. The romantic story of Aïda is based on an actual event in which an Egyptian warrior died for the love of a woman who was an enemy of his country.

THE SCRIBE'S LIFE

A young student of 4,000 or 5,000 years ago who was favored enough to become a scribe did not necessarily have a life of ease, yet it was better than that of most Egyptians. The scribe was a distinguished person, and was treated as such, because so few people mastered the ancient writing and knowledge required for such a position.

Part of the advice of an Egyptian father written to his son about 2000 B.C. was, "Understand that I am putting you in school for your own good. A scribe never knows poverty, and from his childhood is greeted with respect."

Scribes studies included religion, mathematics, medicine, business, and many other kinds of knowledge related to life in those ancient days. However, boys who became scribes were advised to "love writing, hate dancing, and not set their hearts on playing," and, they were warned, "keep away from beer and girls." How fortunate it is that viewpoints differ these days!

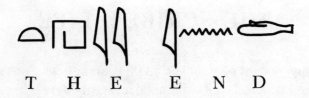

THE END